GW01402934

Original title:

The Pajama Parade to Slumberville

Author: Vivian Laurent

ISBN HARDBACK: 978-9916-90-396-4

ISBN PAPERBACK: 978-9916-90-397-1

The Twilight Comforters

As twilight falls, the shadows blend,
Whispers soft, the day must end.
In gentle hues, the night unfolds,
Embracing dreams, a tale retold.

Stars appear, like diamonds bright,
Guiding souls through velvet night.
In serene silence, hearts align,
Wrapped in peace, like aged wine.

The moonlight dances on the ground,
A silver shroud, a tender sound.
With every sigh, the world feels small,
In twilight's arms, we find our all.

Rest in comfort, close your eyes,
In this realm where stillness lies.
The stars will watch; the night will keep,
Guarding dreams as we drift to sleep.

Cuddle in the Celestial Realm

In the skies where stardust swirls,
We find a haven, a place for girls.
A cosmic hug, the universe wide,
In this embrace, we joyfully glide.

Nebulas bloom in colors rare,
As gentle breezes tease the hair.
Floating softly, lost in grace,
We cuddle close in this vast space.

Galaxies twirl, they call our name,
A dance of light, a cosmic game.
Wrapped in love that knows no bounds,
In this realm, pure magic surrounds.

So hold me tight, here we reside,
In the celestial realms, side by side.
Where dreams are woven from cosmic streams,
Cuddling softly, we'll share our dreams.

Cozy Nightmarch of the Sleepbound

As twilight whispers, the march begins,
Softly gliding, it pulls us in.
The sleepbound souls, in majestic rows,
Under the stars, the nighttime glows.

With every step, the rhythm's slow,
Cradled by night, where dreams will flow.
Shadows trailing, a peaceful grace,
In cozy warmth, we find our place.

The moonlight guides us with its glow,
Leading hearts where soft winds blow.
In this journey, dreams take flight,
Through cozy realms of pure delight.

So follow me, where nightbeats pound,
In this sacred space, we're sleepbound.
Together we wander, hand in hand,
In the cozy night, in dreamland's land.

The Great Escape to Snoozeville

In the twilight's gentle glow,
Dreams begin to ebb and flow.
Clouds of comfort, soft and light,
Guide us through the velvet night.

With a yawn, we drift away,
To a land where shadows play.
Whispers chase the fading day,
In Snoozeville, we long to stay.

Pillows beckon, curtains sway,
As we find our place to lay.
Mirth and laughter fill the air,
In the dreams, we're free from care.

A world where all our wishes gleam,
Awakening the sweetest dream.
In this haven far and wide,
Sleep's embrace, our loyal guide.

Adventures in Flannel and Fantasy

In flannel soft, we take our flight,
Into the realm of stars at night.
With moonlit trails, we weave and spin,
Where fantasy's delights begin.

Each thread a tale, each seam a clue,
Of magical lands waiting for you.
In patterns bold, our dreams ignite,
With every stitch, we claim the night.

Through forests deep and mountains high,
We sail on dreams that touch the sky.
With laughter bright and spirits free,
Adventures wait for you and me.

In cozy wraps and warmth profound,
We'll find the magic all around.
Together in our flannel nest,
In dreams, we journey—truly blessed.

Dreamscape Procession

In whispers soft, the night unfolds,
A dreamscape where the magic molds.
Winding paths of starlit gleam,
In a world that feels like a dream.

With each step, the wonders grow,
Through a field of moonlit glow.
Colors dance and shadows blend,
On this journey with no end.

Figures twirl and laughter sings,
As we chase the joy that dreams bring.
A parade of wishes, bright and free,
In this procession, just you and me.

As dawn approaches, we must go,
Yet in our hearts, the dreams will flow.
In slumber's arms, we find our place,
Forever bound in dreamscape's grace.

Nighttime Journey in Cozy Threads

In cozy threads, the night begins,
With whispered tales and gentle spins.
Underneath a blanket's fold,
We venture where the dreams are told.

With every stitch, a journey starts,
Through lands that dance and touch our hearts.
We roam on paths, both brave and new,
Where skies are bright and dreams come true.

Laughter echoes, shadows play,
In sleepy towns where wishes stay.
Adventure blooms in every seam,
In this embrace, we chase a dream.

So let us wander, hand in hand,
Through the nighttime's wonderland.
In cozy threads, we'll find our way,
And scent of dreams will never stray.

Sleepy Serenity Strut

In twilight's calm embrace, we stroll,
With whispers soft and hearts made whole.
The stars above begin to gleam,
In the hush of night, we weave a dream.

Gentle breezes kiss the trees,
A melody carried on the night's breeze.
Each step a dance through shadowed light,
In sleepy serenity, we find our flight.

The moonlight bathes the world in grace,
Time slows down, a soothing pace.
With every breath, our worries cease,
In this tranquil moment, we find our peace.

Woven Dreams Unfolding

At dusk the fabric starts to weave,
Threads of silver in twilight's reprieve.
Patterns of slumber, softly spun,
A tapestry of dreams begun.

The gentle hum of night fills the air,
With every heartbeat, a whispered prayer.
In shadows, stories come alive,
Woven dreams, where hopes can thrive.

A quilt of memories, stitched with care,
Each patch a moment we gladly share.
In the warmth of night, hearts intertwine,
Together in dreams, your hand in mine.

Tranquil Trek to the Land of Nod

Upon the path where moonlight shines,
We wander through the night's designs.
With every step, the stars align,
A tranquil trek, your heart in mine.

The breeze carries a lullaby's call,
It wraps us tight, a comforting shawl.
Through fields of dreams, we gently glide,
To the land of Nod, side by side.

With whispered secrets and soothing sighs,
We wander beneath the velvet skies.
In this haven, the world fades away,
As dreams unfold at the close of day.

Pajama Pilgrimage of the Hearth

In pajamas soft, we make our way,
Through cozy rooms where shadows play.
With laughter echoing, warmth surrounds,
A pilgrimage where love abounds.

The flicker of candles, a gentle glow,
In this sacred space, our spirits flow.
With every heartbeat, we find our rest,
In the arms of home, we are blessed.

Together we journey through night's embrace,
Finding comfort in each cherished place.
With dreams to share and stories spun,
This pajama pilgrimage is never done.

The Cozy Caravan

Beneath the stars, the caravan sways,
Wrapped in warmth, through night it stays.
With laughter shared, and stories told,
A haven bright, as day turns cold.

The lanterns glow, casting soft light,
In the heart of dusk, it feels so right.
Cushions piled, a comfy nest,
In this small world, we find our rest.

Slumber Sojourn

A journey deep in dreams we take,
Where time drifts slow, and hearts awake.
With gentle whispers, shadows dance,
In tender realms, we find our chance.

The moonlight guides, a silver beam,
In slumber's grasp, we chase the dream.
Each heartbeat echoes, soft and low,
In realms of peace, our spirits glow.

Hibernation Hub

In winter's hold, where warmth resides,
The hibernation hub abides.
Cocooned in soft and silent air,
We gather close, without a care.

The crackling fire and gentle sighs,
Wrapped in blankets, warmth complies.
In dreams we wander, far and wide,
In this snug lair, we bide our time.

The Dreamers' Procession

In twilight's grace, the dreamers move,
With hearts alight, their hopes improve.
Each vision bright, like stars above,
Together they march, with peace and love.

A whisper soft, they share their song,
In unity, they all belong.
Through fields of gold, and skies of blue,
The dreamers march, their journey true.

Tucked In Parade

Little dreams dance in the night,
Whispers of joy taking flight.
Balm for souls, a gentle cheer,
Lullabies wrapping us near.

Stars above twinkle and shine,
In this moment, all is fine.
Cradled in a soft cocoon,
Happiness sings like a tune.

Pillows plush, the world's a blur,
Echoes of peace gently stir.
Under covers, hearts align,
In the warmth, all things divine.

Morning waits with open arms,
While night holds on to its charms.
Tucked in dreams, we drift away,
In the dance of sweet array.

Nurtured in Night's Embrace

Shadows weave a silky thread,
Carrying whispers as we tread.
In the quiet, secrets flow,
As night cradles us below.

Moonlight spills its silver grace,
Drawing hearts to a soft place.
Every sigh, a soft caress,
Nurtured here, we find our rest.

Dreams take form, so rich and bright,
Growing strong in the deep night.
Life's soft lull, a calm escape,
In the warmth of starlit drape.

Here we gather, safe and sound,
In this hush, love is profound.
Nurtured by the night so deep,
Wrapped in warmth, we gently sleep.

Sleepy Spirits' Tribute

In the hush, the spirits sigh,
Songs of peace drift softly by.
Sleepy whispers fill the air,
A tribute to the night so rare.

Gentle shadows hold their ground,
Lulling dreams that soon abound.
Stars nod gently, calm and bright,
Guiding paths through the soft night.

Each thought wrapped in tender care,
Floating free, like whispered air.
Sleepy spirits, take your flight,
Honoring the magic of night.

In the still, we find our way,
Tracing dreams till break of day.
Sleepy spirits, kind and true,
Gift the night, embrace anew.

Softly Stitched Slumber

Fabrics of night softly blend,
In this world where dreams suspend.
Stitched with care, our thoughts entwine,
In the warmth of sleep's design.

Threads of silver, woven bright,
Wrap us close in gentle light.
Every stitch, a lullaby,
Sewing peace as moments fly.

Beneath the quilt of night we lay,
Skyward wishing dreams to sway.
Softly stitched by moon's pure glow,
In the slumber, love does grow.

As the dawn begins to creep,
We awaken from our sleep.
Softly stitched, our dreams reside,
In the heart where hopes abide.

Pajama Quest Under Starlit Skies

Under the stars, we lay in our dreams,
Soft whispers of night, like gentle moonbeams.
In cozy pajamas, we drift and we sway,
Lost in the magic of this peaceful ballet.

With laughter and joy, we chase our delight,
A quest for the dreams that adorn the night.
Each twinkle above, a story untold,
As our hearts weave adventures, both daring and bold.

Knit and Nurture Expedition

In soft woolen threads, our tales intertwine,
Knit with the warmth of affection divine.
We gather the yarns, each color aglow,
Crafting a journey where love starts to flow.

As needles click softly, we share our heart's song,
In this nurturing space, we truly belong.
With every stitch made, a bond starts to form,
An expedition of comfort, through life's gentle storm.

Dreamy Footsteps in Night Attire

Through moonlit paths, our footfalls hum sweet,
In night attire, we dance to the beat.
With stars as our guide, we wander the skies,
Embracing the dreams where our spirit can rise.

In pajamas of wonder, we roam free and bold,
With stories of starlight and mysteries told.
Each step that we take, a journey so rare,
In this dreamy night, we find treasures to share.

Nightwear Odyssey to the Stars

With hearts full of wishes, we set out tonight,
In nightwear we cherish, our spirits take flight.
An odyssey beckons, the cosmos aglow,
As we follow the starlight, wherever it flows.

Through galaxies wide, our laughter does ring,
In pajamas we sail on the laughter of spring.
Hand in hand we travel, no worries, no fears,
Together we'll soar, beyond laughter and tears.

Dream Weavers in Twilight

In twilight's grasp, dreams take flight,
Whispers of stars, shimmering light.
Threads of hope in fabric spun,
Weaving the night, till day is done.

Soft murmurings in the cool air,
Hearts entwined in a gentle care.
Every sigh a wish released,
In the silence, our souls feast.

Minds drift through the silken haze,
Lost in moments, a timeless phase.
With every pulse, the night expands,
As dreams bloom in unseen strands.

In this twilight, we softly glide,
On currents where the shadows bide.
Together, we chase the moon's glow,
As dream weavers dance and flow.

Nighttime Odyssey in Cozy Attire

Wrapped in warmth, we roam the night,
In cozy attire, hearts feel light.
A journey through the velvet dark,
Where whispers echo, and starlights spark.

The world outside drifts far away,
In soft pajamas, we choose to stay.
With mugs of warmth and laughter near,
Each moment spent, a treasure dear.

As dreams unfold on gentle wings,
The nighttime calls, and softly sings.
We wander through the realms of sleep,
In cozy layers, our secrets keep.

Together we traverse the skies,
Beneath the watchful, dreaming eyes.
In this odyssey, we find delight,
Wrapped in comfort, we own the night.

Slumber's Journey Through Starry Streets

Beneath a sky of midnight blue,
Slumber's journey calls us two.
Through starry streets, we drift and sway,
In the realm where night dreams play.

Glimmers of silver, they light our way,
Guiding us through the path of play.
Each step gentle, hearts afire,
Wrapped in dreams that never tire.

Whispers of twilight, secrets unfold,
In this a world of tales retold.
As shadows dance, we softly glide,
On waves of slumber, side by side.

Together we wander, hand in hand,
In starry realms, we take our stand.
Slumber's journey, a tender embrace,
In these streets, we find our place.

The Sleepy Procession of Comfort

In the hush of night, we slowly move,
A sleepy procession, finding our groove.
Wrapped in comfort, a blanket of dreams,
Flowing softly like murmuring streams.

Each step whispers a lullaby sweet,
A dance of peace, in our hearts, we meet.
With stars as lights in the velvet sky,
We journey forth, no need to fly.

Cuddled close, in shadows we share,
Silent stories woven with care.
In every yawn, a promise to keep,
As we wander through the arms of sleep.

A gentle rhythm, the night's own song,
In the realm of comfort, we belong.
The procession moves with a soothing grace,
Embraced by dreams, we find our place.

Swaying Through Sleepy Land

Whispers of the night do call,
Gentle breezes, soft and small.
Stars appear, a twinkling show,
In sleepy land where dreams do flow.

Moonlight dances on the grass,
As shadows fade and moments pass.
Crickets sing a lullaby,
Underneath the velvet sky.

Waves of slumber softly crash,
As evening glows and daylight's ash.
Wrapped in warmth, the world does cease,
In this realm, we find our peace.

Swaying through the dreams we weave,
In this magic, we believe.
Resting lightly, hearts in tune,
Embraced beneath the silver moon.

Moonbeam March to the Daydreams

Through the fields of thought, we stride,
With moonlight as our gleaming guide.
Each step whispers tales untold,
In the night where dreams unfold.

Glittering paths of softest glow,
Lead us where the wild winds blow.
Sailing on a cloud of wishes,
Beneath the sky, our spirit swishes.

Every shadow plays a part,
Casting echoes in the heart.
As we wander, side by side,
In daydreams' arms, we gently glide.

With each moonbeam's tender touch,
We find solace, oh so much.
Marching forth, our dreams embrace,
In this journey, finding grace.

The Soft Landing of Nightwear

In pajamas, soft as a sigh,
We drift like clouds in the sky.
The night calls us to slow our pace,
In cozy corners, we find our place.

Wrapped in blankets, we unwind,
Gently leaving the day behind.
Stars peek in to say hello,
While our feelings start to flow.

With whispered dreams on the air,
The night cradles us in its care.
Floating softly through shadowed dreams,
Life is stitched with silver seams.

As eyelids flutter, spirits soar,
In the stillness, we crave more.
The soft landing of nightwear's grace,
Leads us to our secret space.

Cozy Evening Expedition

In the glow of twilight's gloom,
We embark, dispelling room.
With lanterns bright, our hearts ignite,
On this cozy evening flight.

Through the woods where whispers wane,
Embraced by nature, free of strain.
Each rustling leaf, a secret shared,
In this journey, we are spared.

Warmth of friendship lights the way,
In every laugh, we choose to stay.
With every step, the world feels right,
Together we embrace the night.

Stars above like guardians gleam,
Guiding us through this sweet dream.
In our hearts, we'll hold this spark,
From our cozy evening park.

Duvet Journey Under Moonlight

Beneath the soft, silver light,
Dreams take wing into the night.
Whispers of the stars above,
Guide the heart to peace and love.

As shadows dance upon my face,
I lose myself in this warm space.
The world fades into whispers near,
Wrapped in comfort, free from fear.

Each night a new adventure starts,
With secret paths and wandering hearts.
The moonlit quilt, a guiding hand,
Leads me through this dreamland's strand.

In cozy folds, my worries cease,
Embraced in joy, I find my peace.
The duvet's warmth, my heart's delight,
On this journey under moonlight.

The Comfy Dreamscape Trek

In pajamas soft, I drift away,
To lands where night begins to play.
Cradled in a gentle haze,
I wander through the starry maze.

Each step a twinkle in my mind,
In these dreams, true peace I find.
Comfy clouds beneath my feet,
In this realm, my soul's retreat.

Laughter echoes in the air,
Magic sparkles everywhere.
With every turn, a new surprise,
I chase the wonders in the skies.

On this cozy, dreamscape trek,
I'm free to roam, no need to check.
Wrapped in warmth, I'll drift away,
Till morning breaks the night's ballet.

Pjs and the Night's Whisper

In pajamas snug, I close my eyes,
The night unfolds its softest sighs.
Whispers dance upon my skin,
Inviting dreams to drift within.

The clock ticks softly, time stands still,
Embraced by warmth, I feel the thrill.
Every shadow has a tale,
In this realm where dreams set sail.

Moonlight filters through the seams,
A gentle glow ignites my dreams.
With every breath, the night does sing,
A lullaby the stars do bring.

Pjs hug me close, a tender hold,
In this quiet space, I'm bold.
With every whisper, magic grows,
As I journey where the spirit flows.

Bedtime Revel in Softness

The day has come to sweetly end,
In softness, all my cares transcend.
Under blankets, snug and tight,
I revel in this warm, soft night.

The world outside begins to fade,
In cozy corners, joy is made.
A gentle breeze through curtains sighs,
As dreams emerge from velvet skies.

Each creak and hum, a lullaby,
Inviting me to float and fly.
In this realm, I feel so light,
As wishes take off into the night.

With every breath, I sink and sway,
In this tender dance, I long to stay.
Bedtime whispers, sweet and clear,
A revel in softness, drawing near.

Drowsy Drift into Enchantment

Underneath the silken sky,
Whispers float where shadows lie.
Dreamers walk on starlit streams,
Lost within our quiet dreams.

Softly falls the evening haze,
Twinkling lights begin to blaze.
In this realm where wishes bloom,
We find solace, fade from gloom.

Drifting slowly, heart in tune,
Dancing lightly with the moon.
Every sigh a lullaby,
Carried on the night's soft sigh.

As we weave our tales of night,
Stars ignite our hearts with light.
In this magic, time stands still,
Lost in dreams, we find our will.

The Fabric of Night Adventures

Stitches sewn with silent stars,
Creating paths to worlds afar.
Each thread whispers tales untold,
In this fabric, dreams unfold.

Clouds like sails drift through the air,
Carrying hope without a care.
Underneath the vast expanse,
Every heartbeat finds its chance.

Echoes dance on whispers' breath,
In this night, we flirt with death.
But life ignites in twilight's glow,
As we venture where dreams go.

Stars align in cosmic schemes,
Guiding all our midnight dreams.
In this tapestry of night,
Adventures spark, igniting light.

Twinkling Threads in Slumber

In slumber's arms, we find our nest,
With twinkling threads, the night is blessed.
We weave our dreams with gentle hands,
Creating magic across the lands.

Each star a note in quiet songs,
A lullaby where spirit belongs.
Dancing shadows play and weave,
In the dreams we choose to believe.

Muffled hearts in whispers share,
Secrets wrapped in moonlit air.
As night unfolds its glowing seam,
We drift together, lost in dream.

Tomorrow waits with dawn's embrace,
But in this moment, time finds grace.
Twinkling threads shall guide our way,
In slumber's hold, we choose to stay.

Patterns of Peaceful Dreams

Patterns drawn with softest care,
In peaceful dreams, we learn to share.
Each moment blooms like flowers bright,
Guiding us through tender night.

Gentle waves of starlit glow,
Whispers weaving tales we know.
In the silence, hearts unite,
Lost together in the night.

Clouds of comfort wrap us tight,
On a journey into light.
With every breath, we drift and sway,
In dreams of peace, we find our way.

Beneath the quilt of endless skies,
Hope and joy begin to rise.
Patterns formed by hearts that yearn,
In peaceful dreams, we gently burn.

Slumberwood Journey

In the hush of twilight's grace,
Gentle whispers softly trace,
Paths of dreams in twilight's bloom,
Glide through night's enchanting room.

Stars like lanterns softly gleam,
Guiding souls through realms of dream,
Each step taken, light as air,
Carried forth without a care.

Moonlit streams in shadows play,
Crickets sing the night away,
Woodland creatures hush their cheer,
As we wander, free from fear.

Morning whispers on the brink,
Crimson hues in silence sink,
As we leave this slumbered wood,
With hearts aglow, forever good.

Serene Silhouettes in the Night

Silhouettes dance in soft moonlight,
Casting shapes upon the night,
Whispers sigh through leaves of oak,
Hushed secrets that the shadows cloak.

Stars align, a cosmic guide,
In this calm, our fears subside,
A tapestry of dark and light,
Painting dreams that take their flight.

Glimmers twinkle, piercing skies,
As time flows in gentle sighs,
Night enfolds us, sweet embrace,
In its quiet, we find grace.

Each breath a moment, soft and deep,
Where dreams awaken from their sleep,
In serene silhouettes we find,
A timeless peace for heart and mind.

The Fabric Paradise

Threads of gold and silken strands,
Woven tight by unseen hands,
In this paradise, colors blend,
Creating dreams that never end.

Patterns dance like floating leaves,
Whispers of what the heart believes,
Every stitch a tale retold,
In the warmth of the fabric's fold.

Softly draped on gentle skies,
A tapestry where time complies,
Embraced by threads of love and light,
In this haven, all feels right.

With each turn of fate's own loom,
Magic lingers in this room,
As dreams are spun in softest hue,
In the fabric paradise, we renew.

Dreamy Digression of the Nightwear

Wrapped in fabrics soft and bright,
Embers glow in cozy light,
With every thread, a story spun,
In nightwear dreams, our hearts are one.

Pajamas whisper tales of yore,
Explorations just beyond the door,
Slumber beckons with its call,
In this moment, we embrace it all.

Curtains drawn, the world outside,
In this space, our dreams collide,
Under covers, warm and tight,
Journey forth into the night.

Stitch by stitch, we drift away,
Finding peace where worries sway,
In dreamy digression, we find peace,
In nightwear's embrace, sweet release.

Slumber's Serenade in Fuzzy Fancies

In dreams we float on clouds of care,
Soft whispers call, as night takes air.
Fuzzy fancies wrap us tight,
Guiding us to restful night.

Stars twinkle softly in the dome,
While shadows dance within our home.
The moonlight glows on tranquil seas,
Cradling hearts in gentle breeze.

Pillows hug and blankets sigh,
Cocooned whispers as we lie.
In the silence, magic blooms,
As sleep descends in cozy rooms.

Sleepy eyes begin to close,
Embracing dreams where love just grows.
In the hush, our souls take flight,
In slumber's serenade tonight.

The Nighttime Procession of Snuggles

Gentle night, the world on pause,
A rally of dreams, deserving applause.
Snuggles gather, warm and bright,
In the twilight's soft embrace tonight.

Pajamas fluffed like clouds above,
A tapestry woven with care and love.
Tiny giggles around us dance,
In this moment, hearts find their trance.

Beneath the stars, we come together,
Wrapped in warmth, no stormy weather.
Laughter echoes, a sweet refrain,
Embraced in joy, we feel no pain.

The night unfolds its velvet wings,
In this sanctuary of whispered things.
As the world sleeps, we softly hum,
In the nighttime, we are one.

Enchanted Evening of Nightwear

In twilight's glow, our laughter stirs,
Dressed in dreams, like playful furs.
Whisking us to realms unknown,
In enchanted nightwear, we have grown.

The glow of stars, a silver sheen,
Casting magic where we convene.
Each garment whispers tales untold,
Of adventures bold in twilight's fold.

Slumber charms with every thread,
As cozy fantasies weave and spread.
Soft embraces, warm and light,
Cradle us softly into the night.

In sweet repose, we find our peace,
A soothing balm that will not cease.
In nightwear's embrace, the dreams will flow,
Where wonders live and wishes grow.

Rhythm of the Restful Realm

As night descends, a gentle beat,
The rhythm calls, inviting sweet.
Crickets sing a lullaby,
In the restful realm, we drift and fly.

With every breath, a calming wave,
Together here, the bond we save.
Moonlit glances softly gleam,
Within this space, we share our dream.

Blankets rustle, whispers blend,
In this rhythm, hopes ascend.
A melody of hearts that soar,
Together, we need nothing more.

With open arms, the night does bless,
Rest and peace, a soft caress.
As time stands still, in sweet refrain,
We dance along in joy unchained.

Twilight Wandering in Comfy Wear

In cozy yarns, we drift along,
Soft whispers of the evening song.
Beneath the skies where stars align,
We weave our dreams, both yours and mine.

The world is dimmed, yet hearts are bright,
Wrapped in warmth, we crave the night.
With every step, we leave behind,
The cares of day, so unconfined.

Footsteps light on paths we seek,
In this embrace, our spirits speak.
Twilight dances, gently sways,
In comfy wear, we find our ways.

Together we roam, hand in hand,
Through twilight's glow, a magic land.
With laughter soft, we take our flight,
In comfy wear, we own the night.

Hushed Hues of Nighttime

The night descends with softest grace,
A velvet cloak, a warm embrace.
In shadows deep, the whispers blend,
As day retreats, where dreams transcend.

With muted tones, the world subdues,
In hushed hues, the heart renews.
Stars twinkle in the endless dome,
Guiding us gently to our home.

The moonlight spills a silver trace,
On silent paths, we find our pace.
A lullaby of night sings sweet,
In hushed hues, our dreams compete.

As eyelids droop and softly weigh,
In night's embrace, we drift away.
Through hushed hues, our spirits fly,
In nighttime's arms, we dream and sigh.

Journey Through Bedtime Boulevard

Down Bedtime Boulevard, we roam,
In twilight's glow, we feel at home.
Fairy lights twinkle, guiding the way,
As we wander through the close of day.

Each step we take, a soft delight,
Underneath the blanket of night.
Stories whisper in the breeze,
Inviting us to rest with ease.

The moon hangs low, a watchful friend,
On this journey that will never end.
With gentle dreams, we dance along,
In slumber's arms, we find our song.

As stars align above our heads,
We follow trails where magic spreads.
On Bedtime Boulevard, hearts are free,
In dreamlike realms, we long to be.

The Sleepy Saunter

In gentle steps, we make our way,
The sleepy saunter ends the day.
With hazy thoughts that drift like clouds,
We weave between the evening crowds.

Soft whispers float on twilight's air,
A cozy feel, we have to share.
The world is wrapped in a soft sigh,
As day waves gently, bidding goodbye.

With each soft step, we shed our cares,
In the stillness, find solace there.
A bedtime tale, a lullaby,
As stars awaken in the sky.

The sleepy saunter leads us near,
To dreams where all is bright and clear.
In twilight's grip, we find our peace,
In sleepy wanderings, our joys increase.

Whispers of Wool and Cotton

In fields where colors blend and sway,
Soft fibers dance beneath the day.
Cotton's kiss and wool's embrace,
Nature stirs in a gentle grace.

The threads of stories woven tight,
Each stitch a whisper, pure delight.
Hands of care and love unwind,
A tapestry of dreams we find.

Through cozy nights and sunlit morns,
The warmth of craft in hearts is born.
In every fold, a tale retold,
With wool and cotton, treasures unfold.

So let us wear this soft array,
In whispers of love, we find our way.
For in these fibers, we are drawn,
Together blending, dusk till dawn.

Lullaby Lane Explorers

Down Lullaby Lane where dreams softly sigh,
Adventurers gather, with stars in their eyes.
Each step is a story, each giggle a song,
In the heart of the night, where the brave feel strong.

With lanterns alight, we wander and play,
In fields of imagination, we dance and sway.
Where shadows turn friendly and dreams take their flight,

We explore the vast canvas of shimmering night.

Our laughter a melody, bright stars align,
On this mystical journey, the moonlight will shine.
With every new trail, new wonders await,
Together we roam, through the garden of fate.

So come take my hand, we'll venture and roam,
In the heart of our dreams, we shall always find home.
With joy as our compass, we'll chart our own way,
In the magic of night, we forever will play.

Fleece-Footed Adventures

In the morning haze where dew drops cling,
Fleece-footed friends hear the wildbirds sing.
Paws gently padding on soft, grassy beds,
With whispers of joy in the paths that we tread.

Through forests and valleys, our laughter will soar,
Every twist and turn brings adventures galore.
We leap through the meadows, a joyous parade,
In the heart of the wild, our spirits won't fade.

With each fleeting moment, the world feels so bright,
We chase dreams and shadows, our hearts full of light.
As the sun dips low and the stars start to gleam,
We gather our stories, like pearls on a stream.

So here's to the journeys with friends by our side,
Fleece-footed adventures, in laughter we glide.
To the calls of the wild and the paths we explore,
In memories made, we forever adore.

Moonlit Garb Gala

Beneath the glow of a silvered sphere,
The moonlit gala draws us near.
In shimmering fabrics, we dance and twirl,
With each flowing step, we set hearts a-whirl.

Adorned with stars, our outfits gleam bright,
As whispers of magic fill up the night.
In laughter and song, we celebrate all,
Every stitch a memory at this grand ball.

The night air is filled with stories anew,
As friends gather close under skies deep and blue.
Each twinkle a promise, each sparkle a dream,
Together we sail on this moonlit stream.

So let's raise a toast to the joy we create,
In this beautiful gathering, we dance and weate.
For life is a gala, with love as our theme,
In our moonlit garments, we live out the dream.

Pajama Promenade of the Moon

In soft twilight, we stroll along,
With stars above, a shimmering song.
Pajamas wrapped, a cozy embrace,
The moonlight dances, a gentle grace.

Each step we take, the night feels right,
Whispers of dreams in silver light.
A serene path beneath our feet,
In this haven, our hearts find beat.

With every glance, horizons gleam,
In the fabric of our shared dream.
The world outside fades from view,
In this moment, just us two.

Together we roam, hand in hand,
In the land of dreams, so vast, so grand.
The moon guides us through the night,
In our pajama promenade, delight.

Slippers and Stars Expedition

With slippers on, we venture far,
Chasing trails of every star.
An expedition, calm and light,
Through the canvas of the night.

The universe whispers secrets low,
As we wander where starlit winds blow.
Cushioned footsteps, soft as air,
In this journey, we are rare.

Galaxies twinkle, inviting us near,
In intrigue, we shed every fear.
Exploring realms of cosmic dreams,
Together we flow, like silver streams.

The night unfolds like a cherished scroll,
Each star a wish, each wish a goal.
In slippers and warmth, we glide and soar,
On this expedition, forevermore.

Clothbound Dream Quest

In a quilt of whispers, we entwine,
Within soft threads, our dreams align.
A clothbound quest through realms unknown,
In every stitch, our love has grown.

With every fold, a story we weave,
Adventures cherished, we dare to believe.
The fabric's warmth, it holds us tight,
Guiding our journey through the night.

Tales of wonder, like stars above,
In this quest, we discover love.
Each patch a memory, vivid and bright,
In the tapestry forged by moonlight.

Together we sail on dream's soft sea,
Bound by cloth, it's just you and me.
With hearts aglow, our spirits zest,
In this clothbound dream, we find our rest.

Restful Ramble Through Dreamscapes

As shadows gather, we take our time,
In dreamy realms, where thoughts rhyme.
A restful ramble, slow and sweet,
Through landscapes where the heart can meet.

Echoes of laughter, whispers of peace,
With every step, our worries cease.
Clouds like pillows, soft and white,
In this journey, our souls take flight.

Surreal meadows, blooms of gold,
In this vivid world, we unfold.
Cascading colors that gently blend,
In every corner, a new friend.

With gentle hearts and open eyes,
We savor magic beneath the skies.
A restful ramble through the night's gleam,
Together we wander, forever dream.

Festival of the Sleepy Silhouettes

In shadows long, we gather here,
Soft whispers dance, a night so dear.
With every sigh, the stars take flight,
Embracing dreams in soft moonlight.

Blankets wrapped, we sway and sway,
As quiet thoughts drift far away.
In the hush, our eyes do gleam,
We float upon the waves of dream.

Silhouettes in gentle grace,
Resting in this sacred space.
With each breath, we find our bliss,
In the night's sweet, tender kiss.

The festival of silent hearts,
Where slumber's magic softly starts.
In unity, we close our eyes,
And wander off to starry skies.

Twilight Adventure in Comfy Clothing

As twilight falls, the world transforms,
In comfy clothes, our spirit warms.
We step outside, the air is still,
With every laugh, we find a thrill.

The evening brings a playful breeze,
Amongst the trees, we feel at ease.
In cozy threads, our hearts unite,
In this soft glow of fading light.

We wander paths where shadows play,
And gather memories on the way.
In friendship's fold, we spin and twirl,
As night unfurls its velvet swirl.

With starlit skies, the journey's bold,
In comfy wear, our tales are told.
Together we chase the night away,
In twilight's magic, we laugh and sway.

Nightwear Journeys to Dreamland

In nightwear soft, we close our eyes,
To sail away on whispers, skies.
With stars as guides, we drift and float,
On gentle waves, our dreams emote.

Each cozy stitch holds tales untold,
Of fairies, knights, and treasures bold.
In slumber's hold, we find our peace,
As moments dance, our worries cease.

The moonlight glows on faces sweet,
As dreamland paths we softly meet.
In pajama cloak, our spirits soar,
Through realms unknown, forevermore.

Nightwear journeys, magic streams,
In quiet realms, we weave our dreams.
With heartbeats soft, our souls entwined,
In dreamland's embrace, pure joy we find.

The Cozy Quest of the Dreamers

We launch our quest on pillows high,
With dreamers' hopes that touch the sky.
In cozy nooks, our laughter rings,
As twilight breathes, our spirit sings.

Together we tread on starlit lanes,
Through fields of silver, where joy reigns.
With each step, new worlds unfold,
As tales of wonder we dare to hold.

Wrapped in warmth, our spirits rise,
In search of stars, beyond the skies.
With cozy hearts, we journey forth,
In dreamers' light, we find our worth.

The cozy quest, our hearts aligned,
In every dream, new paths we find.
Amidst the night, we gleam and gleefully roam,
In unity, we carve our home.

Nightwear Journeys to Dreamland

In nightwear soft, we close our eyes,
To sail away on whispers, skies.
With stars as guides, we drift and float,
On gentle waves, our dreams emote.

Each cozy stitch holds tales untold,
Of fairies, knights, and treasures bold.
In slumber's hold, we find our peace,
As moments dance, our worries cease.

The moonlight glows on faces sweet,
As dreamland paths we softly meet.
In pajama cloak, our spirits soar,
Through realms unknown, forevermore.

Nightwear journeys, magic streams,
In quiet realms, we weave our dreams.
With heartbeats soft, our souls entwined,
In dreamland's embrace, pure joy we find.

The Cozy Quest of the Dreamers

We launch our quest on pillows high,
With dreamers' hopes that touch the sky.
In cozy nooks, our laughter rings,
As twilight breathes, our spirit sings.

Together we tread on starlit lanes,
Through fields of silver, where joy reigns.
With each step, new worlds unfold,
As tales of wonder we dare to hold.

Wrapped in warmth, our spirits rise,
In search of stars, beyond the skies.
With cozy hearts, we journey forth,
In dreamers' light, we find our worth.

The cozy quest, our hearts aligned,
In every dream, new paths we find.
Amidst the night, we gleam and gleefully roam,
In unity, we carve our home.

Twilight Comfort Caravan

The caravan rolls in, a journey begins,
With cozy attire, the warmth never thins.
Lanterns aglow, casting soft light,
In twilight's embrace, everything feels right.

Flannel and fleece, like clouds we embrace,
In this comfort zone, we take our place.
Through laughter and stories, the night unfolds,
In our twilight caravan, adventure beholds.

Cozy Ventures into Dreamland

With each little step, we wander and glide,
In pajamas so soft, our dreams coincide.
Each whisper of night, a gentle caress,
In the realm of slumber, we find our rest.

Swaying in rhythm, like leaves in the breeze,
Comfort surrounds us, bringing sweet ease.
Ventures into dreamland, we savor and weave,
In the heart of the night, it's magic we believe.

Nightwear Carnival

In twilight's embrace, the colors unfold,
Silks and satins, stories retold.
Dancing shadows with laughter and cheer,
Whispers of dreams, as night draws near.

Moonlit paths adorned in delight,
Each garment a treasure, sparkling bright.
Stars twinkle above, a celestial view,
The carnival calls, enchanting and true.

Enchanted Sleepwear Soiree

Glimmers of magic in evening's attire,
Whimsical patterns that never tire.
Soft melodies float through the air,
As night weaves its spell, without a care.

Whispers of dreams line the softest sheets,
With every twirl, the heart gently beats.
In robes of wonder, we gather and play,
At the soiree where dreams come to stay.

Furling Fabrics of Fantasy

In twilight's glow, the fabrics weave,
Threads of magic, hearts believe.
Colors dance, in whispers bright,
Magic tales take flight at night.

Gossamer dreams in shadows flow,
Stitching stories, soft and slow.
Patterns twirl, they interlace,
In this realm, we find our place.

Silken wishes in the air,
Furling softly, panel's share.
Every fold, a secret told,
In ethereal hues, so bold.

Underneath the starry dome,
These fabrics weave our dreams of home.
A tapestry of hope displayed,
In the night, our fears allayed.

Pajama Dreams Unveiled

In silky hues, the night unfolds,
Dreams wrapped tight, like stories told.
Cotton clouds in slumber's bliss,
With every sigh, a whispered kiss.

Pajama tales in soft embrace,
Where gentle laughter finds its place.
Starlit nights invite the roam,
In cozy threads, we feel at home.

The moonlight beams through fabric seams,
Casting shadows of our dreams.
With every toss and every turn,
In these pajamas, passions burn.

Drifting softly, night unfolds,
A canvas of dreams, bright and bold.
Pajama dreams, so sweetly stitched,
In cozy warmth, our hearts arewitch'd.

Dream Gathering in Night Attire

Gather 'round in night attire,
Where whispers float and hearts conspire.
Satin slips and flannel hugs,
Dreams ignite like firebugs.

Moonlit gatherings, tales to share,
In cozy quirks, we find our flair.
Each fabric tells of joy and cheer,
In this embrace, the world feels near.

A tapestry of laughter's sound,
In gentle folds, our hopes are found.
Though darkness calls, we feel so light,
In night attire, we own the night.

With every stitch, a bond we weave,
In dreams together, we believe.
As morning dawn breaks the spell,
In night attire, all's well.

Homeward Bound in Cozy Warmth

With every step, the hearth draws near,
Wrapped in warmth, we shed our fear.
A cozy nook awaits our rest,
Homeward bound, we feel the best.

Fireside whispers, tales retold,
In knitted throws, our hearts enfold.
Chocolate sips and laughter bright,
In home's embrace, we find our light.

The winter chill may bite outside,
But in our hearts, love does abide.
Nestled deep in woven care,
Homeward bound, nothing can compare.

Every corner, memories gleam,
In cozy warmth, we chase a dream.
Together here, our lives entwined,
In homeward bound, our peace we find.

The Slumbering Stroll

Beneath the stars, we wander slow,
In whispers soft, where shadows flow.
The moonlight guides our gentle way,
As night unfolds, we drift and sway.

With sleepy eyes, our dreams take flight,
Each step a dance, through velvet night.
The world a hush, in sweet embrace,
A tranquil walk, a sacred space.

The breeze, a sigh, of tales untold,
In every step, a memory holds.
With hearts entwined, we find our peace,
In slumber's grace, we find release.

As dawn approaches, colors bloom,
Our stroll now ends, dispelling gloom.
Yet in our hearts, the night will stay,
In dreams we'll walk, till break of day.

Midnight March of the Dreamers

In shadows deep, the march begins,
A gathering of whispered sins.
With each soft step, the night we claim,
The stars our guide, no two the same.

A silent pact with dreams anew,
Beneath the skies, a vibrant hue.
With laughter bright, we chase the dawn,
In twilight's lace, we linger on.

The echoes rise, of hopes and fears,
A melody that stirs the years.
We walk as one, a ceaseless stream,
In midnight's glow, we dare to dream.

And as the night begins to wane,
With every step, we break the chain.
These fleeting hours, in heart we'll keep,
The midnight march, through dreams we leap.

Soft Fabric Odyssey

In threads of gold, our journey weaves,
A tapestry of hopes and leaves.
Each fiber spun from tales untold,
In whispered dreams, we find our gold.

Through silken paths, we glide along,
With every stitch, we craft a song.
Pausing where the colors blend,
In this embrace, our souls mend.

The fabric flows, a river wide,
In every fold, the world our guide.
From dusk till dawn, we'll roam and play,
In soft embrace, we drift away.

And when the journey finds its close,
In every thread, our love still glows.
This odyssey of fabric bright,
In gentle hands, we weave the night.

Twilight Tapestry Walk

Under the veil of twilight's grace,
We walk through shadows, time's embrace.
The colors fade in gentle sighs,
As starlit whispers fill the skies.

With every step, the world anew,
In twilight's frame, our dreams come true.
The path adorned with twilight's hue,
A journey shared, just me and you.

The golden threads of day now fray,
Yet in our hearts, the light will stay.
Through dusk's soft glow, we find our peace,
In twilight's arms, our spirits cease.

As night unfolds, we drift apart,
But carry with us, every heart.
This tapestry of time we'll weave,
In memories, we shall believe.

Feathered Dreams on Soft Trails

In the whisper of dawn, feathers take flight,
They dance through the skies, hearts feel so light.
Soft trails beneath, where shadows will play,
Dreams weave together in the light of the day.

Gentle breezes hum, as the world awakes,
Nature's lullaby in the morning breaks.
With each step we take, hope begins to grow,
Feathered dreams guide us, wherever we go.

Sunrise painting colors, a canvas so wide,
Soft trails invite us, with love as our guide.
We follow the path where the wildflowers sway,
In feathered dreams, we'll always stay.

As daylight fades softly, stars start to gleam,
We journey together, lost in the dream.
With laughter and whispers, the night comes alive,
On feathered dreams, forever we'll thrive.

Slumberville Soiree in Comfy Garb

In cozy attire, we gather around,
Where pillows and laughter embrace with pure sound.
Slumberville calls, with its warm, gentle light,
A soiree of dreams in the stillness of night.

Blankets like rivers, draped soft on the floor,
Whispers of stories, we long to explore.
Cookies and cocoa, sweet treats shared with glee,
In comfy garb, we're joyful and free.

As shadows play tricks in the glow of the moon,
We sing soft, sweet songs, a comforting tune.
With friends gathering near, our hearts intertwine,
In Slumberville's warmth, all worries decline.

The night is a canvas, painted with cheer,
In comfy attire, we hold moments dear.
As dreams take their flight, we embrace the unknown,
In Slumberville's magic, we find our true home.

The Twilight Retreat

In twilight's embrace, we seek a retreat,
Where shadows grow long and day feels complete.
Whispers of crickets in the soft evening air,
Nature's sweet chorus, a melody rare.

The sun bids goodbye, painting skies with gold,
Creating a tapestry, majestic and bold.
We wander with purpose, beneath starlit skies,
In twilight's calm glow, our spirits arise.

Each step feels like magic, as moments align,
With memories brewing like rich vintage wine.
In twilight's soft arms, we dance with the night,
A retreat of our souls, where everything's right.

As darkness unfolds, dreams softly ignite,
In the twilight's embrace, we feel pure delight.
Together we linger, till dawn's early break,
In this sacred retreat, our hearts gently wake.

Gentle Night Stroll Through Comfort

With every soft step, the world slows its pace,
We stroll under stars, in this tranquil place.
Gentle night whispers, like secrets they share,
In comfort we wander, with dreams in the air.

The moonlight illuminates paths we will find,
With love in our hearts, and peace in our mind.
Each shadow a promise, each breeze a soft sigh,
As we walk through the night, just you and I.

The stars twinkle softly, a guiding light beam,
In this gentle night stroll, we live in a dream.
The world sleeps around us, in sweet, silent grace,
In comfort we'll cherish this magical place.

As night bids farewell and dawn starts to gleam,
We carry the peace, like a warm, friendly seam.
Gentle night strolls provide memories rare,
In comfort, forever, our hearts will compare.

Serenade of the Sleepy Socks

In a drawer where shadows dwell,
Soft and warm, they weave a spell.
Colors mingled, patterns bright,
Whispering secrets of the night.

Dancing lightly on the floor,
Footsteps soft, a gentle roar.
They curl up, no more to roam,
In cozy corners, they find home.

Under blankets, snug and tight,
Socks embrace the dreams of night.
As moonlight drapes with silver thread,
They cradle all the thoughts we've fed.

Morning calls, they start to wake,
With each stretch, the world they take.
Together, ready for the day,
Sleepy socks will find their way.

Twilight Tapestry of Dreamers

Beneath the stars, where shadows blend,
Dreamers gather, hearts to mend.
Whispers glide on breezy air,
Creating tales beyond compare.

With every breath, the night unveils,
A tapestry of ancient tales.
Threads of silver, gold, and blue,
Weaving hopes, both old and new.

The moonlight paints their dreams so bright,
A canvas stitched with sheer delight.
Together, they drift on the lake,
In unison, their wishes wake.

As dawn peeks from the curtain's edge,
They promise to hold their pledge.
In twilight's arms, they find their peace,
Until the day's soft magic cease.

The Cozy Caravan of Night

Rolling gently, wheels delight,
Cradled in the arms of night.
Stars are lanterns, shining bright,
Guiding dreams in cozy flight.

Through the valleys, whispers flow,
Tales of places, we do not know.
Laughter echoes, shadows play,
In this caravan, joy holds sway.

Every mile, a story spun,
Underneath the watchful sun.
Crickets sing, as fires glow,
While the world outside moves slow.

Hitch your heart, let worries cease,
Find your rhythm, feel the peace.
In this cozy, roving nest,
The magic of the night is best.

Chasing Clouds in Dreamy Garb

Through the sky, we float and glide,
In our dreams, we cast aside.
Draped in fabric soft as air,
Chasing clouds without a care.

Whirling gently on the breeze,
Laughing lightly, hearts at ease.
Twirling shapes of white and grey,
Guiding us along the way.

With every sigh, the stars align,
In this realm, our spirits shine.
Wrapped in visions, bold and free,
We become the dreams we see.

As dawn breaks, the clouds will fade,
Leaving traces of the parade.
Yet in our hearts, they linger near,
Chasing dreams, we hold so dear.

Wandering in Woven Wonders

In fields of fabric, colors blend,
Threads of stories, hand in hand.
Through patterns rich, my heart does mend,
In woven wonders, dreams expand.

A tapestry of hopes unspun,
Each stitch a whisper, soft and clear.
I chase the daylight, warmth of sun,
Leaving behind the weight of fear.

Around each corner, magic stirs,
Textures dance in gentle sway.
A world alive with whispered purrs,
In woven realms, I long to stay.

With each step taken, I am free,
Embracing colors, light, and sound.
In this crafted sanctuary,
The heart of art is truly found.

The Dreamscape Expedition

In the realm where visions grow,
Night's canvas glimmers, vast and wide.
Guided by stars, soft winds do blow,
On waves of dreams, we gently glide.

Through portals bright, we twirl and spin,
With every heartbeat, time stands still.
Discoveries awaits within,
As wanderlust ignites the thrill.

Unraveling wonders, shadows greet,
A dance of light in every hue.
With open minds, we feel the heat,
The spark of magic, brave and new.

As dawn approaches, visions fade,
Yet memories linger, soft and sweet.
A dreamscape's promise, unafraid,
Awaits our return, life's grand repeat.

Pajama Carnival Beneath the Stars

Under the blanket, soft and snug,
Dreamers gather, laughter bright.
Pajamas on, we dance and hug,
Beneath the stars, our hearts take flight.

With popcorn dreams and stories shared,
A carnival of giggles gleams.
In cozy worlds, we are unpaired,
The night ignites our wildest dreams.

Each twinkling light, a friend in sight,
Whispers of joy in shadows cast.
We twirl with glee in shared delight,
Creating memories that will last.

As moonbeams paint our swirling hearts,
In every corner, magic glows.
In this embrace where love imparts,
The pajama carnival softly flows.

Nocturnal Retreat in Silken Swirls

A velvet night in silken swirls,
Wraps around, a calming shroud.
With soothing whispers, gently unfurls,
A retreat where dreams are loud.

The stars ignite with soft caress,
A journey through the calm and deep.
In twilight's touch, we find our rest,
In sorrows, joy and secrets keep.

Each moment drapes like satin fine,
Cradling hearts in quiet grace.
In this embrace, the world declines,
And peace unfolds in every space.

As dawn approaches, we awake,
Yet traces linger, soft and sweet.
In silken swirls, memories make,
A tapestry of dreams complete.

Pajama Carnival Beneath the Stars

Under the blanket, soft and snug,
Dreamers gather, laughter bright.
Pajamas on, we dance and hug,
Beneath the stars, our hearts take flight.

With popcorn dreams and stories shared,
A carnival of giggles gleams.
In cozy worlds, we are unpaired,
The night ignites our wildest dreams.

Each twinkling light, a friend in sight,
Whispers of joy in shadows cast.
We twirl with glee in shared delight,
Creating memories that will last.

As moonbeams paint our swirling hearts,
In every corner, magic glows.
In this embrace where love imparts,
The pajama carnival softly flows.

Nocturnal Retreat in Silken Swirls

A velvet night in silken swirls,
Wraps around, a calming shroud.
With soothing whispers, gently unfurls,
A retreat where dreams are loud.

The stars ignite with soft caress,
A journey through the calm and deep.
In twilight's touch, we find our rest,
In sorrows, joy and secrets keep.

Each moment drapes like satin fine,
Cradling hearts in quiet grace.
In this embrace, the world declines,
And peace unfolds in every space.

As dawn approaches, we awake,
Yet traces linger, soft and sweet.
In silken swirls, memories make,
A tapestry of dreams complete.

Whispering Shadows of Sweet Dreams

In the hush of night's embrace,
Shadows dance with gentle grace.
Whispers float on breezes light,
Carrying secrets through the night.

Stars above with soft glow shine,
Painting dreams as hearts align.
A lullaby that softly flows,
In the world where silence grows.

Moonbeams weave a silver thread,
Into every thought we spread.
Every sigh and silent plea,
Unraveled in tranquility.

As darkness wraps around the earth,
Each moment feels like a rebirth.
Whispering shadows gently tread,
Into the realms where dreams are fed.

Flannel Fantasia Under Moonlight

Wrapped in warmth of flannel tight,
Underneath the soft moonlight.
Each corner filled with laughter's call,
A tapestry where dreams enthrall.

The world outside fades away,
In this cozy, sweet array.
Flickering candles cast their glow,
On memories that ebb and flow.

Beneath the stars, stories unfold,
In soft whispers, tales are told.
Every hug a gentle sway,
Carried through the perfect day.

A flannel night, so calm and still,
With every heartbeat, every thrill.
In this fantasia, we reside,
Under the moon, forever tied.

Soft Threads and Starlit Sky

In the loom of night's embrace,
Soft threads weave a sacred space.
Underneath the starlit sky,
Whispers of the past drift by.

Patterns formed in timeless grace,
Captured in this velvet place.
A tapestry of dreams portrayed,
Where every hope and wish is laid.

With each thread, a tale unfolds,
Of love and laughter, stories told.
Woven gently, side by side,
In the fabric where we abide.

Stars above like diamonds gleam,
Threads of life intermix and seam.
Underneath that vast expanse,
We find our hearts in night's romance.

Midnight Stroll in Dreamy Robes

In robes of dreams, we take a stroll,
Through the night, we find our soul.
Whispers call from shadows deep,
Inviting us to drift and leap.

Twinkling stars, our guiding light,
In the dark, we feel so right.
With every step, the world unfolds,
A tapestry of stories told.

The moon hangs low, a silver crest,
As we wander, feeling blessed.
Each moment shared in peace divine,
In the midnight hour, hearts entwine.

Dreamy robes that softly sway,
Carrying our cares away.
In the magic of this night,
We find our path, our hearts take flight.

Cuddle Parade Under the Moon

In the glow of silver light,
Soft whispers fill the night.
Wrapped in warmth, we snuggle tight,
Hearts dancing in pure delight.

Stars twinkle like our dreams,
Gentle laughter, soft moonbeams.
Together, we craft our schemes,
In this world of starlit themes.

Each embrace a tender song,
In this place, we both belong.
Through the night, we glide along,
In the magic, we grow strong.

Cuddle tight, let worries fade,
In our cozy, sweet parade.
Under moonlight, love displayed,
In this moment, unafraid.

Fuzzy Footprints Through Fantasy

In a land where dreams unfold,
Fuzzy footprints, stories told.
Magic whispers soft and bold,
In this wonder, hearts turn gold.

Through the meadows, laughter sways,
In the warmth of sunny rays.
Every step, a dance that plays,
Chasing dreams in joyful ways.

Clouds like candy in the sky,
With each giggle, spirits fly.
Exploring realms where wishes lie,
Together, we both reach high.

Fuzzy footprints mark our quest,
In this journey, find our rest.
Hand in hand, we feel so blessed,
In this dream, we are the best.

Nighttime Comfort Crusade

Under blankets, cozy tight,
We embark on dreams tonight.
Soft the shadows, peace in sight,
In this stillness, hearts take flight.

Whispers weave a gentle tale,
Every thought, a soothing sail.
Stars above, our nightingale,
Guiding us when hopes prevail.

With each heartbeat, calm and clear,
Nighttime wraps us, draws us near.
In this comfort, shed each fear,
Together, love's the souvenir.

Every sigh, a lullaby,
Underneath the moonlit sky.
In this moment, we both lie,
Breathing dreams, just you and I.

Restful Roaming Through Twilight

As dusk unfolds its gentle hand,
We wander through this dreamland.
With every step, we understand,
In this calm, our hearts expand.

Twilight paints the earth so bright,
Shadows dance, a soft delight.
In this hush, with love in sight,
We find solace, pure and right.

The world around us softly sighs,
With every breath, the night complies.
Underneath the starlit skies,
Together, our spirits rise.

Restful roaming, hand in hand,
In this magic, we both stand.
Through the twilight's tender band,
Love encircles, sweet and grand.

Starlit Strolls in Soft Fabrics

Beneath the velvet sky so bright,
We walk in whispers, hearts take flight.
In silken threads, we glide and weave,
Embracing night, we shan't deceive.

The moonlight dances on our skin,
While gentle breezes call us in.
In shadows deep, our secrets grow,
As starlit dreams begin to flow.

In cozy wraps, we share our tales,
As twilight's hush, our spirit hails.
Each step a rhythm, soft and sweet,
A melody where moments meet.

So here we linger, hand in hand,
In softest fabrics, love we've planned.
With every gaze toward the night,
Our starlit strolls forever bright.

A Voyage of Dreams in Nighty Garb

In nighty garb, we drift away,
To lands where soft whispers play.
Our dreams set sail on silver streams,
Guided by the light of beams.

The stars above, our compass true,
Through velvet skies, we wander through.
With every heartbeat, visions spin,
In twilight realms, our journey begins.

With every sigh, the worlds unfold,
In twilight's embrace, our stories told.
In fabric soft, our spirits glide,
On this voyage, we confide.

Together, we dance on celestial shores,
In dreams and nighties, forever we'll soar.
This journey boundless, sweet as night,
In love's soft embrace, our hearts take flight.

Slumber's Soiree Under the Stars

As twilight falls, the stars awoke,
A soiree blooms, in dreams bespoke.
Under a canopy of night,
We gather warmth, hearts burning bright.

With cozy throws and laughter shared,
In slumber's grips, we're softly paired.
The moonlight wraps us in a hug,
As whispers float like a gentle mug.

Each twinkling light a tale to tell,
In dreams of wonder, we cast our spell.
With every yawn, our eyelids droop,
In slumber's soiree, we find our loop.

Together we drift, entwined in peace,
As night's embrace grants sweet release.
With every breath, we weave our scene,
In starry slumber, our hearts convene.

Tucked In Tales from the Dreamers

Tucked in tight, with stories spun,
From dreamers' hearts, adventures run.
In blankets soft, we whisper low,
Of distant lands where loved ones glow.

Each tale a thread, a tapestry,
Of magic realms, where minds run free.
With every turn and twist of fate,
In dreams we find our secret gate.

From dragons fierce to stars that gleam,
In vivid hues, we chase our dream.
As morning breaks, we'll hold them fast,
These tucked-in tales forever last.

So come, dear friend, let's close our eyes,
And journey far beneath the skies.
In slumber's arms, we'll weave our song,
Tucked in with tales where we belong.

9 789916 903964